THE DELUSIONAL POET

Poems of a Dreamer

KANIKA PRAKASH

BookLeaf Publishing

India | USA | UK

To my parents and my savior - SHIVA.

Acknowledgment

A heartfelt thank you to BookLeaf Publishing for bringing my first book to life and giving me the opportunity to turn my dream into reality. Your belief in my work has been truly invaluable.

To my family— especially my parents and my brother— whose unwavering love and support have been the foundation upon which I stand.

To my close friends, for being my constant source of joy, encouragement, and strength. Your faith in me, even in moments of doubt, has meant more than words can express.

To the courage within me that refused to let me stop, and to God, for guiding me through this journey.

And finally, to you, the readers, for joining me in this adventure—thank you for making it all worthwhile.

Preface

From the bustling streets of Delhi to the serene heights of the Himalayas, my journey has been one of exploration, both within and beyond. As a lawyer and a feminist, I've navigated the intricate corridors of justice, advocating for equality and mental health awareness. Writing has been my constant companion since my days in law school at eighteen, offering solace and a medium to voice the unspoken.

"Womeniaa," my blog, has been a sanctuary where stories of resilience, empowerment, and the complexities of womanhood took shape. Through poetry, I have ventured deeper into these themes, capturing both the transient and the eternal, the whispered and the unsaid.

This collection is a tapestry woven from my experiences—each poem is a reflection of moments spent in quaint cafés, days lost in the mountains, and the silent wars fought in the mind. It is a testament to living unapologetically, unshackled by societal judgments.

I am profoundly grateful to BookLeaf Publishing for believing in my vision and transforming this dream into reality. Their support has been instrumental in transforming these poems from the recesses of my heart to the pages before you.

May these poems resonate with you, offering comfort, inspiration, and a reminder that our journeys, though unique, are beautifully intertwined.

KANIKA PRAKASH
womeniaa.blogspot.com.

Rani: A Symphony of Strength and Grace

I'M FLAWED LIKE WHISKEY,
RAW AS BURNED COAL,
TOUGH AS STONE,
SOFT AS SPUN COTTON,
SWEET AS CARAMEL,
BITTER AS VIRGIN MOJITO.
BUT ABOVE ALL,
I'M A DARLING, FOR SURE
MY OWN BESTIE
FULL OF DESIRES.
SMELL AS LAVENDER,

BUT POLITICS WITHIN
HEAD-TO-TOE CHAOS,
BUT A HEART MADE OF GOLD,
A WOMAN OF CLASS,
WITH A LOVE FOR WINE,
AND A FIRE THAT NEVER FADES.

DELHI KA ISHQ-
दिल्ली का इश्क़

पुरानी दिल्ली जैसा इश्क़ मांग रही हूँ,
छत पे सूखाए हुए अचार सी महक हो जिसमें,
करोल बाग की गलियों सी गूंज,
चांदनी चौक की चाट सा तीखापन,
किसी पुराने किले की ढलती शाम का सुकून,
लोधी गार्डन में हाथों में हाथ वाली वॉक,
चाय और समोसे सा मेल मांग रही हूँ।
दिल्ली से हूँ, दिल मांग रही हूँ।

Description - The poem expresses a longing for the unique experiences and the soul of

Delhi. It's a poetic tribute to the city's character and the emotional ties one can have with a place that is not just a location but a feeling.

Whispers of Desire

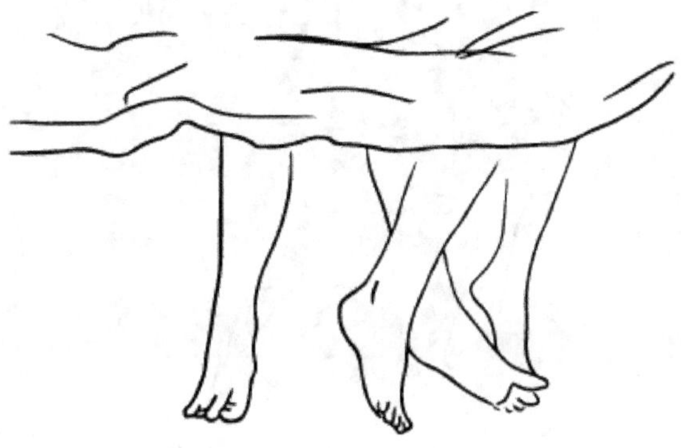

To cosmic heights, my love does soar,
A bond eternal, forevermore.
A celestial embrace, pure and bright,
A love so tender, a breathtaking sight.
Soft whispers, secrets, a lover's plea,
Let passion's fire ignite, untamed and free.
I'll bend and yield, to your every desire,
A love so fervent, a soul set afire.

ISHQ-E-RUKHSATI -
इश्क-ए-रुखसती

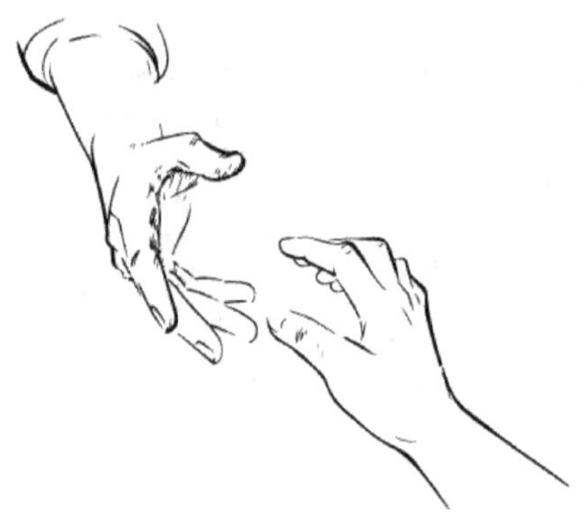

रुखसती में भी जो तेरी बंदगी का एहसास है,
तेरे इश्क का वो आलम खूबसूरत सा,
मेरी रूह तेरी बेहिसाब मोहब्बत की डोर में बंधी
इस क़दर,
तू एक मुलायम सा खिलता गुलाब है,
बक़दर तेरे अल्फाज़ हैं,
कि तेरी रुखसती भी मेरे ज़ेहन में इश्क-ए-आगाज़
है।
कि तेरी रुखसती भी मेरे ज़ेहन में इश्क-ए-आगाज़
है।

Description - This poem, "Ishq-e-Rukhsati" (इश्क़-ए-रुखसती), explores the enduring power of love even during separation. The poet expresses how, despite the farewell, the feeling of devotion and the beauty of the lover's affection remains ever-present. Some words and phrases are described as;

1\.   रुखसती – Separation
2\.   बंदगी – Devotion
3\.   आलम - Universe
4\.   बक़दर – Worthy
5\.   आगाज़ - Start

In Your Arms

Be the dream that lingers in your waking
sight,
The shining light that guides your way.
Let's plunge into your heart's deep night,
And in your arms, forever stay.
Hand in hand, let's wander home,
Where love's sweet feast we'll cook with care,
With flavors of romance, let's freely roam,
A perfect story, we'll share.
Our title "Us."

WAR OF INK -
जंग-ए-स्याही

हमारे तो फ़साद भी कलम से लड़े जाते हैं,
तलवारें तुम्हारी बहती होंगी लहू,
हमारी तो कलम की स्याही बहती देख,
ना फ़सादों का ज़िक्र भूल गए, तो कहना।
कर लो तुम अपनी तलवारों से जंग,
हमसे उलझे तो जीत हमारी स्याही की होनी तय
है।

Description - This poetry contrasts the power of intellect and ideas (symbolized by the pen) with the force of violence (symbolized by the sword). It suggests that while opponents may use physical power and bloodshed, the poet's battle is fought through words and discourse.

The Unwritten Chapter

You're the verse that falters,
Lost in a poem's embrace,
A chapter left unread,
A subject that's out of grace.
A playlist paused forever,
A love story's unfinished sigh,
A theory half-conceived,
A tale where dreams refuse to fly.
You're the missing piece,
The puzzle's empty space,
The half-told story,
The unfinished embrace.

Depth -गहराई

सफ़र ये नहीं है आसान, मंज़िल तक की एक चाह है,,
किनारों पे ठहरी हुई, ख़ामोश एक नाव है।
गहरा कितना ये रास्ता है, ये तो सफ़र की लहरों का तकाज़ा है,
न जाने कितनी तेज और ये लहरें हमें मंजिल तक पहुँचने से रोक पाएगी।
क्या पता कल फिर कोई नाव हमें मंजिल से मिला दे।

Description - The poem portrays life as a challenging journey across deep and turbulent waters, symbolizing struggles and uncertainties. The "नाव" (boat) represents hope and resilience, while the "लहरें" (waves) reflect obstacles. Despite the unpredictable depth of life's path, the poet conveys optimism, emphasizing perseverance and the possibility of unexpected help leading to success.

Soft Bloom

Diamonds may gleam, a hardened grace,
But flowers whisper, love's embrace.
Gold I'll buy, a prize well-earned,
"Lovedigger" blooms, a sweeter word.
No tears shall flow, a river's plight,
But love's sweet stream, a pure delight.
Ice cream shared, a simple bliss,
No wedding wealth, no gilded kiss.

Like romcom scenes, a gentle sway,
But "Radha" passion, come what may.
Hashtags bloom, a love's sweet art,
No "Vibha + Rajan = Vibhajan" tears shall
rend apart.
A touch of cringe, a human touch,
Love's imperfect loved so much.

DARKNESS- अँधेरा

उजाले में भी अंधेरा लगता है,
साँस भी अब ज़हरीली लगती है।
बूंद-बूंद पानी सी हवा हो गई है,
बाहर कदम निकलने पर अब भय होता है।
चारों ओर बस सन्नाटा पसरा हुआ दिखता है,
मौत तो जैसे खेल हो गई हो।
आज साँस चलती है, तो कल का डर लगता है,
अपनों को अलविदा न कह पाने की चुभन भी।
पर इस सब का जिम्मेदार आपको कौन लगता है?
पता लगे तो बताना, मैं यूँ ही फिर कुछ लिख
दूँगी।
कल शायद अंधेरे में भी उजाला दिख जाए।

Description - This poem poignantly reflects
the fear, isolation, and uncertainty that

defined the COVID-19 pandemic. It captures the eerie silence, the ever-present anxiety of losing loved ones, and the suffocating reality of a world where even air felt toxic. Through its verses, the poet encapsulates the shared human experience of loss, helplessness, and the lingering hope that even in darkness, light may one day return.

The Sea's Farewell

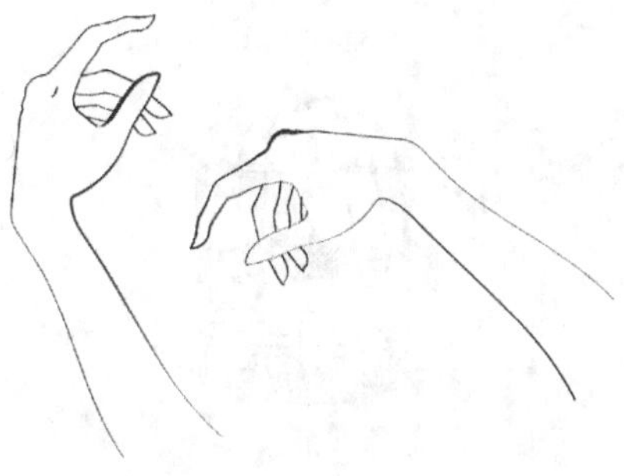

The ocean's kiss, a gentle hand,
As life's long journey meets the sand.
A peaceful sleep, a quiet rest,
A soul released, eternally blessed.

OLD SCHOOL - विंटेज

टिंडर के इस जमाने में, चिट्ठी से गुफ़्तगू करने
वाला इश्क़ चाहिए।
सारी रात वीडियो कॉल नहीं, बस घंटों बैठकर
मुशायरों वाली बात चाहिए।
2024 में, मिलेनियल या जेन Z नहीं, बस विंटेज
वाला प्यार चाहिए।

Description - This poem expresses a longing
for an old-fashioned, deep love, contrasting
with the fast-paced, technology-driven world
of today. The Poet yearns for heartfelt
communication, like writing letters and
having meaningful conversations, rather than
relying on quick, superficial interactions.

Measure - पैमाना

उसने कहा, "शराब सा नशा किसमें है?"
मैंने कहा, "इश्क़ किया होता, तो शराब का नशा
फीका लगता ।"
उसने कहा, "फिर इश्क़ करूं या शराब से यारी?"
मैंने कहा, "एक दिन अकेले बैठना,
दो ग्लास लेकर, एक में अपने लिए शराब भरना,
और एक ख़ाली छोड़ देना मेरे इश्क़ के लिए।"
फिर देखेंगे, नशा कौन से ग्लास में है—
तुम्हारी शराब में या मेरे इश्क़ के ख़ाली ग्लास में।

Description - The poem compares the intoxication of love with that of alcohol. The poet suggests that if the person had experienced love, the effect of alcohol would seem insignificant.

Literature- लेख

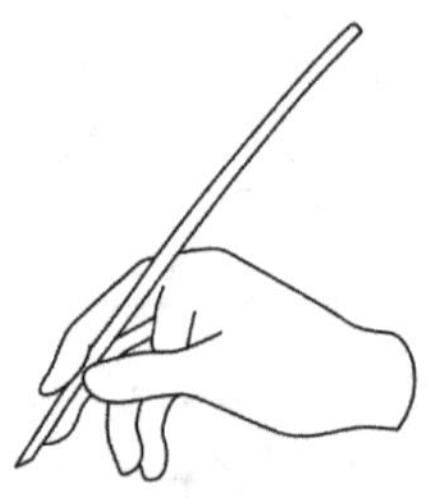

शायरी भी मैं,
ग़ज़ल भी मैं,
नज़म भी मैं,
कविता भी मैं।
मैं अपनी ही कहानी हूँ,
किसी भी किताब में छुपा,
वो उपन्यास भी मैं।
वो उस गीत का गीतिकाव्य भी मैं,
लेखक का शब्द हूँ,
मैं एक लेख हूँ और लेखक भी।

Description - Literature is an art that can express every aspect of humanity through words. Whether it is poetry, ghazal, nazm, or a novel, each form of literature holds its charm and significance. Through writing, an author shares their thoughts, emotions, and experiences, which not only tell the story of their own life but also reveal a broader perspective of society.

FIRST LOVE – पहला प्यार

तू जो लौट कर आया है,
पर शर्ता सा है।

लब तेरे कुछ कहते हैं,
और आँखों में कुछ बूंदें हैं मेरे इश्क़ की,
अब बता
फिर से जाने को आया है,
या इस बार मुकम्मल करनी है,

ये पहेली मोहब्बत की।

Description - This poetry expresses the complex emotions of love. The poet reflects on a love that has returned, but with conditions, that make it uncertain. The poet questions whether this return is another departure or if this time, the love will be fully realized and completed, solving the mystery of their relationship. It's a poetic exploration of uncertainty, longing, and the desire for fulfillment in love.

The One - एकय

सुंदर, महेश, नटराज
शक्ति, मुक्ति
अनंत से आदि
सत्य भी, ब्रह्म भी।
एक भी, एकय भी
बनारस के अस्सी घाट की चिता भी।
मुझमें भी, तुझमें भी
दाता भी, विधाता भी
परमात्मा भी, आत्मा भी
शिव काशी, शिव बनारस
शिव मेरा भी
शिव तेरा भी
शिव।

Description - The poetry speaks of Shiva as the absolute, eternal truth and presence in all things—both within and beyond human understanding. It reflects the philosophical concepts of unity, divine essence, and the eternal cycle of life and death.,

The Unknown Destination- अज्ञात मंजिल

जिन्दगी की इस भीड़ में
खुद की ही तो तलाश है,
राहें थोड़ी उदास हैं
मंजिल का पता है,
पर हौसलों की बात है
डर कर इस दुनिया के
तानों से हार का ही
एक एहसास है
तनहाई में भी
बस शोर का ही साथ है।

Description - The poem explores the internal conflict of losing one's way, with a clear destination but obscured by doubt and external pressures. It touches on self-discovery, loneliness, and societal expectations, highlighting the tension between hope and fear.

The Bargain of Dreams -
सपनों का सौदा

दुनिया एक सौदा है,
तु सौदाबाज बन,
पंख फैला और उड़ जा।
तु गीत बन के गुनगुना,
समुद्र बन और सब कुछ अपने अंदर समेट,
तु दिया बन और किसी के घर की रोशनी बन।
रुक, ठहर, सांस ले।
तु तू बन और
कल के खुद को भूल,
चल फिर नया सवेरा बन और जीत ले ये दुनिया।

Description - The poem urges
self-empowerment and transformation, using

metaphors like a song, sea, and lamp to
emphasize spreading positivity and
embracing change. It encourages
introspection, letting go of the past, and
striving for success in the world.

Puzzle -पहेली

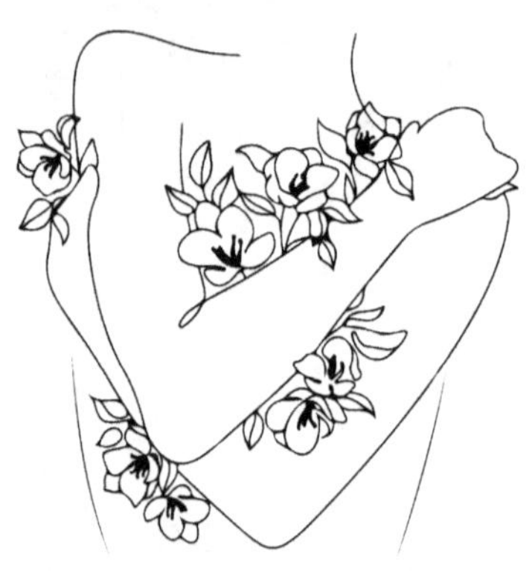

एक पहेली हूँ,
हीरा कोहिनूर हूँ,
शराब की तरह चढ़ती हूँ,
ढलती शाम सा सुकूँ हूँ,
मैं बेशक एक इश्क़ हूँ,
पर कांच सा नाज़ुक भी,
ज़रा नज़र हटी और
टूट कर बिखर जाऊँगी।
नीर, नूर, नारी हूँ,
ज्वाला हूँ पर
नदी सी सरल भी,
मैं बावरी सी
एक अकेली हूँ।
मैं एक पहेली हूँ।

Description - This poem depicts love as a precious yet fragile puzzle, strong like wine, peaceful like the setting sun, and delicate like glass. It combines fiery intensity and simplicity, showcasing love's emotional depth, vulnerability, and paradox of being both powerful and fragile.

NOOR-E-ISHQ - नूर-ए-इश्क़

बेखौफ, बेबाक
आजाद
किसी भी बंदिश
से दूर
बस इक मैं और एक तू
रात चाँद और गुफ्तगू
कुछ क़िस्से में मैं
कुछ किस्सों में तू
मेरा इश्क़
मैं
और तेरा नूर।

Description - The poem conveys a deep, unrestricted love between two people, where they are free from any constraints, sharing intimate moments under the night sky. Their connection is portrayed as a blend of personal experiences, with one person's love and the other's light completing the bond between them.

शेर-ओ-शायरी

1. कमाल करते हो ज़नाब ईश्क़ भी करते हो,
और उसे बदनाम भी करते हो।
या तो उसे यूँ बदनाम न करो या फिर,
खुद उससे बदनाम हो जाओ।

2. ईद मुबारक उस चाँद को भी जो
ना ईद को दिखा न मेरे दिल-ए-दीद को।

To be continued

शेर-ओ-शायरी

3. मैंने तुझे उस नजर से भी देखा है
जिससे दुनियां कभी सोच भी न सकी।
पर कम्बक्त उस नज़र से भी तू मेरा न हुआ।

4. क़या ग़ालिब, क़या गुलज़ार हुए,
क़या ग़ालिब, क़या गुलज़ार हुए,
मोहब्बत में डूबे तो हर कोई बर्बाद हुए।

www.ingramcontent.com/pod-product-compliance
Lightning Source LLC
La Vergne TN
LVHW051237200726
843510LV00011B/1597